Th

STOIC

Book of

QUOTES

Over 500 Philosophical
Quotations for Inspiration,
Achieving Inner Peace, Resilience,
and Growth in Your Daily Life

*Quotes from Marcus Aurelius, Epictetus, Seneca,
and Other Philosophers*

Michael Whiteclear

The Stoic Book of Quotes
Over 500 Philosophical Quotations for Inspiration, Achieving Inner Peace,
Resilience, and Growth in Your Daily Life
Quotes from Marcus Aurelius, Epictetus, Seneca, and Other Philosophers

Copyright © 2024 by Michael Whiteclear
All rights reserved.

ISBN: 9798873645053

CONTENTS

INTRODUCTION

My journey through Stoic philosophy has led me to fill numerous notebooks and countless sheets of paper with Stoic quotes, each page a testament to the enduring wisdom of this ancient practice. These pages have been my companions, guiding me through various stages of life, and they hold timeless wisdom that is profoundly relevant and beneficial for our modern world.

As someone immersed in Stoicism, I've always found these quotes to be more than just words; they are life lessons, offering insights into finding success, joy, and peace in our tumultuous times. This book is a culmination of this lifelong collection, serving as an excellent supplement to my previous book, *Stoicism for New Life*, on Stoic practices. It's designed to enhance your thinking, broaden your worldview, and help you evolve into the best version of yourself, discovering success, joy, and peace in the process.

This book aims to offer you direct access to the wisdom of Stoicism, making it relevant and easily understandable for you, the modern reader. Whether you're seeking guidance, inspiration, or a moment of reflection, these quotes are here for you. You can open a random page each day for daily inspiration or read through systematically, immersing yourself in the profound depth of Stoic wisdom.

I have conditionally divided the quotes into four parts, each corresponding to one of the Virtues: Wisdom, Courage, Justice, and Temperance. However, it's important to note that this division is conditional. The beauty of Stoic wisdom lies in its universality and adaptability. Many of the quotes in this book transcend a single virtue, resonating with multiple aspects of Stoicism and life itself.

I hope that as you read through these pages, you find not only wisdom and guidance but also a deeper connection to the Stoic way of life. May these quotes inspire you, challenge you, and, above all, help you on your journey to becoming the best version of yourself.

WISDOM

THE VIRTUE OF WISDOM

Imagine navigating life with a compass that always points you toward clarity, insight, and understanding. That compass is wisdom, the first of the four cardinal virtues in Stoicism. It's not just about knowing; it's about how you apply that knowledge in the real world. Wisdom is the art of living according to reason and making choices that align with the natural order of things.

At its core, wisdom in Stoicism is about seeing things as they truly are, unclouded by personal biases or emotional reactions. It's the ability to discern what is essential and what is not, to focus on what is within your control, and to let go of what isn't. Wisdom is the virtue that enables you to navigate life's complexities with a clear mind and a steady heart.

THE PRACTICALITY OF WISDOM

Stoicism teaches us that wisdom is deeply practical. It's not just theoretical knowledge or philosophical musings; it's about applying these insights in your daily life. Whether dealing with personal challenges, professional decisions, or interpersonal relationships, wisdom guides you to respond with reason and understanding.

So, how do you cultivate this essential virtue? It starts with self-reflection and a commitment to lifelong learning. It's about curiosity, asking questions, and being open to new perspectives. Wisdom grows from a willingness to learn not just from books and teachers but from every experience and every interaction.

A key aspect of wisdom is rational thinking. It's about using logic and reason to guide your decisions rather than being swayed by fleeting emotions or external pressures. This doesn't mean suppressing your emotions; rather, it's about understanding them, learning from them, and not letting them dictate your actions.

Life is unpredictable and constantly changing. Wisdom involves being adaptable and flexible, understanding that what worked yesterday might not work today. It's about being resilient in the face of change, learning to flow with the currents of life rather than resisting them.

Every day presents opportunities to practice wisdom. It might be in how you handle a difficult conversation, your choices about your health and well-being, or how you respond to unexpected events. Wisdom is about taking a step back, assessing the situation with a clear mind, and making choices that reflect your deepest values and principles.

WISDOM IN YOUR LIFE

As you read through the quotes in this section, reflect on how they resonate with your own experiences. Think about how you can apply these insights in your life. Remember, wisdom is not just about understanding Stoic philosophy; it's about living it. It's about making choices that bring you closer to the person you want to be and the life you want to live.

In conclusion, wisdom is the foundation upon which a Stoic life is built. It's the virtue that guides you toward clarity, understanding, and the right action. As you embark on this journey of wisdom, remember that it's a path, not a destination. Each step you take is an opportunity to grow, learn, and live more fully by your true nature.

"Waste no more time arguing about what a good man should be. Be one."

"No person is free who is not master of himself."

"Where you arrive does not matter so much as what sort of person you are when you arrive there."

"We are not given a good life or a bad life. We are given life, and it's up to us to make it good or bad."

"What we do now echoes in eternity."

"It's not what happens to you,
but how you react to it that matters."
EPICTETUS

"You have power over your mind – not outside
events. Realize this, and you will find strength."
MARCUS AURELIUS

"Some things are in our control
and others not."
EPICTETUS

"Begin at once to live, and count each separate
day as a separate life."
SENECA

"People who labor all their lives but have no
purpose to direct every thought and impulse
toward are wasting their time –
even when hard at work."
MARCUS AURELIUS

"True nobility isn't about being better than someone else; it's about being better than you used to be."

SENECA

"The happiness of your life depends upon the quality of your thoughts."

MARCUS AURELIUS

"Let us prepare our minds as if we'd come to the very end of life. Let us postpone nothing."

SENECA

"First, say to yourself what you would be; and then do what you have to do."

EPICTETUS

"The universe is change; our life is what our thoughts make it."

MARCUS AURELIUS

"How much time he saves who does not look to see what his neighbor says or does or thinks."

MARCUS AURELIUS

"If a man knows not to which port he sails, no wind is favorable."

SENECA

"The soul becomes dyed with the color of its thoughts."

MARCUS AURELIUS

"Only the educated are free."

EPICTETUS

"As is a tale, so is life: not how long it is, but how good it is, is what matters."

SENECA

"The key is to keep company only with people
who uplift you, whose presence
calls forth your best."

EPICTETUS

"Here is a rule to remember in the future, when
anything tempts you to feel bitter: not "This is
misfortune," but "To bear this worthily
is good fortune."

MARCUS AURELIUS

"If you know you are in the right, why fear
those who misjudge you?"

EPICTETUS

"It's not what we say or think that defines us,
but what we do."

SENECA

"Don't mistake your assumptions
for the truth."

EPICTETUS

"Hang on to your youthful enthusiasms – you'll be able to use them better when you're older."

"A key point to bear in mind: The value of attentiveness varies in proportion to its object. You're better off not giving the small things more time than they deserve."

"Prefer enduring satisfaction to immediate gratification."

"Dream big dreams; only big dreams have the power to move men's souls."

"Seek not the good in external things; seek it in yourselves."

"The best way of avenging yourself is by not becoming like the one who wronged you."

MARCUS AURELIUS

"Anger, if not restrained, is frequently more hurtful to us than the injury that provokes it."

SENECA

"Evil is a by-product of forgetfulness, laziness, or distraction: it arises when we lose sight of our true aim in life."

EPICTETUS

"We are more often frightened than hurt; our troubles spring more often from imagination than from reality."

SENECA

"There is only one way to happiness, and that is to cease worrying about things that are beyond the power of our will."

EPICTETUS

"If you're honest, straightforward, and mean well, it should show in your eyes. It should be unmistakable."

MARCUS AURELIUS

"We suffer not from the events in our lives, but from our judgments about them."

EPICTETUS

"There is but one chain holding us in fetters, and that is our love of life."

SENECA

"The first rule is to keep an untroubled spirit. The second is to look things in the face and know them for what they are."

MARCUS AURELIUS

"What difference does it make, after all, what your position in life is if you dislike it yourself?"

SENECA

"Circumstances don't make the man; they only reveal him to himself."

EPICTETUS

"Life, if well lived, is long enough."

SENECA

"Do not be overheard complaining... not even to yourself."

MARCUS AURELIUS

"When someone is properly grounded in life, they shouldn't have to look outside themselves for approval."

EPICTETUS

"If it is not right, do not do it; if it is not true, do not say it."

MARCUS AURELIUS

"Remember how long thou hast already put off these things and how."

MARCUS AURELIUS

"I have learned to see that whatever comes about is nothing to me if it lies beyond the sphere of choice."

EPICTETUS

"Loss is nothing else but change, and change is Nature's delight."

MARCUS AURELIUS

"Life is very short and anxious for those who forget the past, neglect the present, and fear the future."

SENECA

"We are disturbed not by what happens to us but by our thoughts about what happens."

EPICTETUS

"How much more grievous are the
consequences of anger than the causes of it."

MARCUS AURELIUS

"As long as you live, keep learning
how to live."

SENECA

"To enjoy our lives, we must temper our
desires and live within the means of nature,
not of opinion."

ZENO OF CITIUM

"Every new beginning comes from some other
beginning's end."

SENECA

"It isn't possible to change your behavior and
still be the same person you were before."

EPICTETUS

"Luck is what happens when preparation meets opportunity."

SENECA

"The nearer a man comes to a calm mind, the closer he is to strength."

MARCUS AURELIUS

"If you really want to escape the things that harass you, what you need is not to be in a different place but to be a different person."

SENECA

"The more things you examine in the light of reason, the stronger your reason grows – just as feeding more wood to a fire makes it burn brighter and higher."

MARCUS AURELIUS

"For what is just and good is on my side."

MARCUS AURELIUS

"There is no man so fortunate that there shall not be by him something to be looked upon with fear."

SENECA

"Happiness is commonly mistaken for passively experienced pleasure or leisure. That conception of happiness is good only as far as it goes. The only worthy object of all our efforts is a flourishing life. True happiness is a verb. It's the ongoing dynamic performance of worthy deeds. The flourishing life, whose foundation is the virtuous intention, is something we continually improvise, and in doing so, our souls mature. Our life has usefulness to ourselves and to the people we touch."

EPICTETUS

"No one can keep you from living as your nature requires. Nothing can happen to you that is not required by Nature."

MARCUS AURELIUS

"Our greatest blessings come to us by way of
madness, provided the madness
is given us by divine gift."

SENECA

"Do not act as if you had ten thousand years to
throw away. Death stands at your elbow. Be good
for something while you are alive and able."

MARCUS AURELIUS

"The willing are led by fate,
the reluctant dragged."

CLEANTHES

"We should always allow some time to elapse,
for time discloses the truth."

SENECA

"We should not moor a ship with one anchor or
our life with one hope."

EPICTETUS

"He who follows reason in all things is both tranquil and active at the same time, and also cheerful and collected."

MARCUS AURELIUS

"If you accomplish something good with hard work, the labor passes quickly, but the good endures; if you do something shameful in pursuit of pleasure, the pleasure passes quickly, but the shame endures"

MUSONIUS RUFUS

"The soul is our king. If it be safe, the other functions remain on duty and serve with obedience, but the slightest lack of equilibrium in the soul causes them to waver along with it."

SENECA

"First, learn the meaning of what you say, and then speak."

EPICTETUS

"It is not that we have a short time to live, but that we waste much of it."

"No great thing is created suddenly."

"The mind that is anxious about the future events are miserable."

"We should always be asking ourselves: "Is this something that is, or is not, in my control?"

"To enjoy true happiness, we must travel into a very far country and even out of ourselves."

"The tranquility that comes when you stop
caring what they say. Or think or do.
Only what you do."

MARCUS AURELIUS

"There is no genius without a touch
of madness."

SENECA

"What progress, you ask, have I made? I have
begun to be a friend to myself."

HECATO OF RHODES

"The whole future lies in uncertainty:
live immediately."

SENECA

"We should conduct ourselves not as if we
ought to live for the body, but as if we could not
live without it."

MUSONIUS RUFUS

"Happiness and freedom begin with a clear understanding of one principle: Some things are within our control, and some things are not."

EPICTETUS

"Work done with anxiety about results is far inferior to work done without such anxiety, in the calm of self-surrender."

MARCUS AURELIUS

"While we are postponing, life speeds by"

SENECA

"Practice even what seems impossible. The left hand is useless at almost everything for lack of practice. But it guides the reins better than the right. From practice."

MARCUS AURELIUS

"The goal of life is living in agreement with Nature."

ZENO OF CITIUM

"Pleasure is not a reward for virtue,
but virtue itself."

SENECA

"At what time soever thou wilt, it is in thy
power to retire into thyself, and to be at rest, and
free from all businesses."

MARCUS AURELIUS

"The only freedom which deserves the name is
that of pursuing our own good in our own way."

CHRYSIPPUS

"We must give lengthy deliberation to what has
to be decided once and for all."

SENECA

"As the body is to the soul, so is reason to the
spirit. As clothes are to the body,
so is opinion to reason."

MUSONIUS RUFUS

"And even though it is ordained to be, what does it avail to run out to meet your suffering? You will suffer soon enough when it arrives, so look forward meanwhile to better things."

SENECA

"The Fates guide the person who accepts them and hinders the person who resists them."

CLEANTHES

"Let all your efforts be directed to something; let it keep that end in view. It's not an activity that disturbs people, but false conceptions of things that drive them mad."

SENECA

"The condition and characteristic of a sage is that he expects neither benefit nor harm from any external thing."

EPICTETUS

"What really ruins our character is the fact that none of us looks back over his life."

SENECA

"The blazing fire makes flames and brightness out of everything thrown into it."

MARCUS AURELIUS

"Practice yourself, for heaven's sake, in little things, and thence proceed to greater."

EPICTETUS

"We suffer more often in imagination than in reality."

SENECA

"Everything that happens happens as it should, and if you observe carefully, you will find this to be so."

MARCUS AURELIUS

"On Time: Men trifle with the most precious thing in the world, but they are blind to it because it is an incorporeal thing because it does not come beneath the sight of the eyes, and for this reason, it is counted a very cheap thing – nay, of almost no value at all."

SENECA

"Progress is not achieved by luck or accident, but by working on yourself daily."

EPICTETUS

"What is the point of dragging up sufferings which are over, of being miserable now because you were miserable then?"

SENECA

"The lamp of wisdom shines brightest when lit by the flame of self-awareness."

MUSONIUS RUFUS

"To be everywhere is to be nowhere."

"The most important contribution to peace of mind is never to do wrong."

"Begin – to begin is half the work, let half still remain; again begin this, and thou wilt have finished."

MARCUS AURELIUS

"A man is as miserable as he thinks he is."

"When you arise in the morning, think of what a precious privilege it is to be alive – to breathe, to think, to enjoy, to love."

MARCUS AURELIUS

"There are more things to alarm us than to harm us, and we suffer more often in apprehension than reality."

SENECA

"The memory of everything is very soon overwhelmed in time."

MARCUS AURELIUS

"We should not, like sheep, follow the herd of creatures in front of us, making our way where others go, not where we ought to go."

SENECA

"Do not think that what is hard for you to master is humanly impossible, and if it is humanly possible, consider it to be within your reach."

MARCUS AURELIUS

"Nothing is more hostile to a firm grasp on knowledge than self-deception."

ZENO OF CITIUM

"Life is long enough, and it has been given in sufficiently generous measure to allow the accomplishment of the very greatest things if the whole of it is well invested."

SENECA

"To be calm when you've found something going on is a sign of a rational mind."

MARCUS AURELIUS

"Every action should be done in the light of nature's law; it is the harmony between our actions and the law of nature that constitutes virtue."

ZENO OF TARSUS

"Is an emerald suddenly flawed if no one admires it?"

MARCUS AURELIUS

"A life without examination is not worth living. We must continuously scrutinize our actions and motives to ensure they align with our true nature and virtue."

SOCRATES (INFLUENTIAL TO STOIC THOUGHT)

"Your principles have life in them. For how can they perish unless the ideas that correspond to them are extinguished?
And it is up to you to be constantly fanning them into new flame."

MARCUS AURELIUS

"A happy life is one which is in accordance with its own nature."

SENECA

"Think of the life you have lived until now as over and, as a dead man, see what's left as a bonus and live it according to Nature. Love the hand that fate deals you and play it as your own, for what could be more fitting?"

MARCUS AURELIUS

"It is part of the cure to wish to be cured."

SENECA

"To love only what happens, what was destined. No greater harmony."

MARCUS AURELIUS

"Do not wish to be anything but what you are, and try to be that perfectly."

EPICTETUS

"The best way to prepare for life is to begin to live."

MUSONIUS RUFUS

"The object of life is not to be on the side of the majority, but to escape finding oneself in the ranks of the insane."

MARCUS AURELIUS

"It was nature's intention that there should be no need for great equipment for a good life: every individual can make himself happy."

SENECA

"Therefore, nothing ought to be unexpected by us. Our minds should be sent forward in advance to meet all problems, and we should consider not what is wont to happen, but what can happen."

SENECA

"In your actions, don't procrastinate. In your conversations, don't confuse. In your thoughts, don't wander. In your soul, don't be passive or aggressive."

MARCUS AURELIUS

"The things you think about determine the
quality of your mind."
MARCUS AURELIUS

"Life is long if you know how to use it."
SENECA

"If you want something good,
get it from yourself."
EPICTETUS

"When you are disturbed by events and lose
your serenity, quickly return to yourself and don't
stay upset longer than the experience lasts, for
you'll have more mastery over your inner
harmony by continually returning to it."
MARCUS AURELIUS

"The wise man listens to meaning;
the fool only gets the noise."
MUSONIUS RUFUS

"Where, then, lies the mistake, since all men crave a happy life? It is that they regard the means for producing happiness as happiness itself, and, while seeking happiness, they are really fleeing from it."

SENECA

"If someone is able to show me that what I think or do is not right, I will happily change, for I seek the truth, by which no one was ever truly harmed. It is the person who continues in his self-deception and ignorance who is harmed."

MARCUS AURELIUS

"Harmony makes small things grow; lack of harmony makes great things decay."

SENECA

"Better to trip with the feet than with the tongue."

ZENO OF CITIUM

"You always own the option of having no opinion. There is never any need to get worked up or to trouble your soul about things you can't control. These things are not asking to be judged by you. Leave them alone."

MARCUS AURELIUS

"No one becomes a laughingstock who laughs at himself."

SENECA

"The more we value things outside our control, the less control we have."

EPICTETUS

"How ridiculous and how strange to be surprised at anything that happens in life."

MARCUS AURELIUS

"Time heals what reason cannot."

SENECA

"It is better to do wrong seldom and to own it,
and to act right for the most part than seldom to
admit that you have done wrong
and to do wrong often."

EPICTETUS

"Misfortune nobly born is good fortune."

MARCUS AURELIUS

"Life is like a play: it's not the length, but the
excellence of the acting that matters."

SENECA

"Confine yourself to the present."

MARCUS AURELIUS

"If one accomplishes some good though with
toil, the toil passes, but the good remains; if one
does something dishonorable with pleasure, the
pleasure passes, but the dishonor remains."

MUSONIUS RUFUS

"Everything we hear is an opinion, not a fact. Everything we see is a perspective, not the truth."

MARCUS AURELIUS

"Know, first, who you are, and then adorn yourself accordingly."

EPICTETUS

"He who lives in harmony with himself lives in harmony with the universe."

MARCUS AURELIUS

"Your happiness depends on three things, all of which are within your power: your will, your ideas concerning the events in which you are involved, and the use you make of your ideas."

EPICTETUS

"Self-reliance, always. And cheerfulness."

MARCUS AURELIUS

"Time is a sort of river of passing events, and strong is its current; no sooner is a thing brought to sight than it is swept by and another takes its place, and this too will be swept away."

MARCUS AURELIUS

"It is a great thing to know the season for speech and the season for silence."

SENECA

"Don't just say you have read books. Show that through them, you have learned to think better, to be a more discriminating and reflective person. Books are the training weights of the mind. They are very helpful, but it would be a bad mistake to suppose that one has made progress simply by having internalized their contents."

EPICTETUS

"Look back over the past, with its changing empires that rose and fell, and you can foresee the future too."

MARCUS AURELIUS

"We must not believe the many who say that only free people ought to be educated, but we should rather believe the philosophers who say that only the educated are free."

EPICTETUS

"The wise man sees in the misfortune of others what he should avoid."

MARCUS AURELIUS

"Dwell on the beauty of life. Watch the stars, and see yourself running with them."

MARCUS AURELIUS

"We have two ears and one mouth, so we should listen more than we say."

ZENO OF CITIUM

"You become what you give your attention to."

EPICTETUS

"Never let the future disturb you. You will meet it, if you have to, with the same weapons of reason which today arm you against the present."

MARCUS AURELIUS

"No loss should be more regrettable to us than losing our time, for it's irretrievable."

ZENO OF CITIUM

"A man's worth is no greater than the worth of his ambitions."

MARCUS AURELIUS

"Proper preparation for the future consists of forming good personal habits."

EPICTETUS

"To recover your life is within your power; simply view things again as once you viewed them, for your revival rests in that."

MARCUS AURELIUS

"Humanity must seek what is not simple and obvious using the simple and obvious."

MUSONIUS RUFUS

"The same thing, really, that we all want: to live in peace, to be happy, to do as we like, and never be foiled or forced to act against our wishes."

EPICTETUS

"I do what is mine to do; the rest does not disturb me."

MARCUS AURELIUS

"Let us say what we feel and feel what we say; let speech harmonize with life."

SENECA

"Nowhere can man find a quieter or more untroubled retreat than in his own soul."

MARCUS AURELIUS

"Any person capable of angering you becomes your master; he can anger you only when you permit yourself to be disturbed by him."

EPICTETUS

"Be like the cliff against which the waves continually break, but it stands firm and tames the fury of the water around it."

MARCUS AURELIUS

"Attach yourself to what is spiritually superior, regardless of what other people think or do. Hold to your true aspirations no matter what is going on around you."

EPICTETUS

"Then where is harm to be found? In your capacity to see it. Stop doing that, and everything will be fine."

MARCUS AURELIUS

"No man is happy who does
not think himself so."

MARCUS AURELIUS

"You will deserve respect from everyone if you
will start by respecting yourself."

MUSONIUS RUFUS

"Pass then through this little space of time
conformably to nature, and end thy journey in
content, just as an olive falls off when it is ripe,
blessing nature who produced it, and thanking the
tree on which it grew."

MARCUS AURELIUS

"In the morning when thou risest unwillingly,
let this thought be present – I am rising to the
work of a human being. Why, then, am I
dissatisfied if I am going to do the things for
which I exist and for which I was
brought into the world?"

MARCUS AURELIUS

"It is impossible for a man to learn what he thinks he already knows."

EPICTETUS

"We cease to be so angry once we cease to be so hopeful."

SENECA

"We shrink from change, yet is there anything that can come into being without it?"

MARCUS AURELIUS

"Know you not that a good man does nothing for appearance sake, but for the sake of having done right?"

EPICTETUS

"It is quite possible to be a good man without anyone realizing it."

MARCUS AURELIUS

"These reasonings are unconnected: "I am richer than you. Therefore, I am better"; "I am more eloquent than you. Therefore, I am better." The connection is rather this: "I am richer than you. Therefore, my property is greater than yours;" "I am more eloquent than you. Therefore, my style is better than yours." But you, after all, are neither property nor style."

EPICTETUS

"Today, I escaped anxiety. Or no, I discarded it, because it was within me, in my own perceptions – not outside."

MARCUS AURELIUS

"We learn not in the school, but in life."

SENECA

"Whatever time you choose is the right time. Not late, not early."

MARCUS AURELIUS

"I was once a fortunate man, but at some point fortune abandoned me. But true good fortune is what you make for yourself. Good fortune: good character, good intentions, and good actions."

MARCUS AURELIUS

"Nothing is burdensome if taken lightly, and nothing need arouse one's irritation so long as one doesn't make it bigger than it is by getting irritated."

SENECA

"If we were to measure what is good by how much pleasure it brings, nothing would be better than self-control – if we were to measure what is to be avoided by its pain, nothing would be more painful than lack of self-control."

MUSONIUS RUFUS

"Adopt new habits yourself: consolidate your principles by putting them into practice."

EPICTETUS

"This is what you deserve. You could be good today. But instead, you choose tomorrow."

MARCUS AURELIUS

"Nothing is in reality either pleasant or unpleasant by nature, but all things become so through habit."

EPICTETUS

"You need to avoid certain things in your train of thought: everything random, everything irrelevant. And certainly everything is self-important or malicious. You need to get used to winnowing your thoughts so that if someone says, "What are you thinking about?" you can respond at once (and truthfully) that you are thinking this or thinking that."

MARCUS AURELIUS

"We do not need many words, but, rather, effective words."

SENECA

"The happy man is satisfied with his present situation, no matter what it is, and eyes his fortune with contentment."

SENECA

"We must, therefore, take a less serious view of all things, tolerating them in a spirit of acceptance: It is more human to laugh at life than to weep tears over it."

SENECA

"That which is really beautiful has no need of anything; not more than law, not more than truth, not more than benevolence or modesty."

MARCUS AURELIUS

"If you meet temptation, use self-control; if you meet pain, use fortitude; if you meet revulsion, use patience."

EPICTETUS

"Don't explain your philosophy. Embody it."

EPICTETUS

"Expecting is the greatest impediment to
living. In anticipation of tomorrow,
it loses today."

SENECA

"Reason shows us there is nothing either good
or bad, but thinking makes it so."

SENECA

"Give your heart to the trade you have learned,
and draw refreshment from it."

MARCUS AURELIUS

"Those who are well constituted in the body
endure both heat and cold: and so those who are
well constituted in the soul endure both anger and
grief and excessive joy and the other affects."

EPICTETUS

"Look within. Within is the fountain of good, and it will ever bubble up if thou wilt ever dig."

MARCUS AURELIUS

"If you find yourself acting to impress others or avoiding action out of fear of what they might think, you have left the path."

EPICTETUS

"To be free of passion and yet full of love."

MARCUS AURELIUS

"And why should we feel anger at the world? As if the world would notice."

MARCUS AURELIUS

"Follow your principles as though they were laws. Do not worry if others criticize or laugh at you, for their opinions are not your concern."

EPICTETUS

"Truth often harms the one who digs it up."
SENECA

"When you feel burning desire
for something that appears pleasureful, you are
like a person under a spell. Instead of acting on
impulse, take a step back – wait till the
enchantment fades and you can see
things as they are."
EPICTETUS

"No one can steal your peace of mind
unless you let them."
EPICTETUS

"When one is busy and absorbed in one's
work, the very absorption affords great delight;
but when one has withdrawn one's hand from the
completed masterpiece, the pleasure
is not so keen."
SENECA

"Nothing has such power to broaden the mind as the ability to investigate systematically and truly all that comes under thy observation in life."

MARCUS AURELIUS

"The opinion of 10,000 people is of no value if none of them know anything about the subject."

MARCUS AURELIUS

"The mind, when distracted, absorbs nothing deeply."

SENECA

"You can be invincible if you enter into no contest in which it is not in your power to conquer."

EPICTETUS

"To overcome himself, and every day to be stronger than himself."

MARCUS AURELIUS

"From this instant, then, choose to act like the worthy and capable person you are. Follow unwaveringly what reason tells you is the best course."

EPICTETUS

"A man standing by a spring of clear, sweet water and cursing it. Meanwhile, the fresh water keeps on bubbling up. He can shovel mud into it or dung, and the stream will carry it away, wash itself clean, remain unstained."

MARCUS AURELIUS

"It matters not what one says but what one feels; also, not how one feels on one particular day, but how one feels at all times. There is no reason, however, why you should fear that this great privilege will fall into unworthy hands; only the wise man is pleased with his own. Folly is ever troubled with the weariness of itself."

SENECA

"The husbandman deals with the land;
physicians and trainers with the body; the wise
man with his own Mind."

EPICTETUS

"To pursue the unattainable is insanity, yet the
thoughtless can never refrain from doing so."

MARCUS AURELIUS

"And can you be forced by anyone to desire
something against your will? No."

EPICTETUS

"Beautiful things of any kind are beautiful in
themselves and sufficient to themselves. Praise is
extraneous. The object of praise remains what it
was – no better and no worse."

MARCUS AURELIUS

"A great mind becomes a great fortune."

SENECA

"The important thing about a problem is not its solution, but the strength we gain in finding the solution."

SENECA

"Whether he lives a long time or a short time amounts to the same thing, for the present moment is of equal duration for everyone, and that is all any man possesses."

MARCUS AURELIUS

"The road is long if one proceeds by way of precepts but short and effectual if by way of personal example."

SENECA

"All things were ready for us at our birth; it is we that have made everything difficult for ourselves through our disdain for what is easy."

SENECA

"To grieve or be angry about or fear what happens to you is to be a fugitive from the law of nature."

"And there's no state of slavery more disgraceful than one which is self-imposed."

"A man, when he has done a good act, does not call out for others to come and see, but he goes on to another act."

"Because when you engage in the same things as the masses, you lower yourself to their level."

"What is the product of virtue? Tranquility."

"In times of happiness, no point in shaking
things up. But in a time of crisis,
the safest thing is change."

SENECA

"Now is the time to get serious about living
your ideals. How long can you afford to put off
who you really want to be? Your nobler self
cannot wait any longer.

Put your principles into practice – now. Stop
the excuses and the procrastination. This is your
life! You aren't a child anymore. The sooner you
set yourself to your spiritual program, the happier
you will be. The longer you wait, the more you'll
be vulnerable to mediocrity and feel filled with
shame and regret because you know you are
capable of better.

From this instant on, vow to stop disappointing
yourself. Separate yourself from the mob. Decide
to be extraordinary and do what
you need to do – now."

EPICTETUS

"To read with diligence; not to rest satisfied with a light and superficial knowledge, nor quickly to assent to things commonly spoken."

MARCUS AURELIUS

"If you didn't learn these things in order to demonstrate them in practice, what did you learn them for?"

EPICTETUS

"Most of what we say and do is not necessary, and its omission would save both time and trouble."

MARCUS AURELIUS

"It betrays a lack of an interior life when a person is overly focused on bodily things – whether indulging in food and drink, exercising to exhaustion, or spending excessive time on grooming. Care for your body as needed, but put your main energies and efforts into cultivating your mind."

EPICTETUS

"He who has seen the present has seen everything, that which happened in the most distant past and that which will happen in the future."

MARCUS AURELIUS

"Whenever externals are more important to you than your own integrity, then be prepared to serve them the remainder of your life."

EPICTETUS

COURAGE

THE VIRTUE OF COURAGE

Let's explore Courage, a virtue that resonates deeply with our innate desire to face life's challenges head-on. In the Stoic sense, Courage isn't just about heroic acts; it's about the daily bravery required to live true to our principles, even in the face of adversity.

Courage is the strength to act in accordance with our values, regardless of external pressures or internal fears. It's about confronting discomfort, uncertainty, and even pain with a steadfast heart. This virtue is not the absence of fear but the ability to move forward despite it.

CULTIVATING COURAGE IN DAILY LIFE

How do we cultivate Courage in our daily lives? It starts with small steps. Each time we choose to face a fear, speak our truth, or stand up for what's right, we strengthen our courage muscle. It's about recognizing that every challenge is an opportunity to grow and that true bravery lies in the willingness to be vulnerable.

Stoicism teaches us rational Courage. It's not about reckless bravery but a calculated approach to facing life's challenges. It involves weighing our choices, understanding the potential risks and rewards, and then acting in a way that aligns with our deepest values.

Life is inherently uncertain, and change is its only constant. Courage in Stoicism means embracing this reality, not with resignation, but with a proactive mindset. It's about adapting to new situations, learning from them, and finding ways to thrive amidst the unknown.

Every day, we encounter situations that call for Courage. It might be making a difficult decision at work, addressing a personal weakness, or standing up for someone else. Courage is about taking these moments head-on, clearly understanding our values and the outcomes we seek.

YOUR PERSONAL JOURNEY WITH COURAGE

As you delve into the quotes in this section, reflect on how they speak to your life. Think about the areas where you can practice more Courage. Remember, Courage is not about grand gestures; it's about the small, consistent acts of bravery that shape our character and our lives.

In essence, Courage is about living authentically, facing life with an open heart, and embracing each moment as an opportunity to grow. It's a journey of stepping out of our comfort zones, challenging ourselves, and ultimately, becoming the best versions of ourselves. Embrace this path of Courage, and let it guide you to a life of purpose, resilience, and fulfillment.

"Difficulties strengthen the mind,
as labor does the body."

SENECA

"If you are pained by external things, it is not
they that disturb you, but your own judgment of
them. And it is in your power to wipe out
that judgment now."

MARCUS AURELIUS

"He who fears death will never do anything
worth of a man who is alive."

SENECA

"To bear trials with a calm mind robs
misfortune of its strength and burden."

SENECA

"Throw me to the wolves, and I will return
leading the pack."

SENECA

"The art of living is more like wrestling than dancing, for it requires us to stand firm and ready against every unforeseen event."

MARCUS AURELIUS

"He didn't care; it was not his skin he wanted to save, but the man of honor and integrity. These things are not open to compromise or negotiation."

EPICTETUS

"It's not because things are difficult that we dare not venture. It's because we dare not venture that they are difficult."

SENECA

"We often are angry," says our adversary, "Not with men who have hurt us, but with men who are going to hurt us, so you may be sure that anger is not born of injury."

SENECA

"Because a thing seems difficult for you, do
not think it impossible for
anyone to accomplish."

MARCUS AURELIUS

"A gem cannot be polished without friction,
nor a man perfected without trials."

SENECA

"The best revenge is not to be
like your enemy."

MARCUS AURELIUS

"It is not death that a man should fear, but he
should fear never beginning to live."

MARCUS AURELIUS

"Reject your sense of injury, and the injury
itself disappears."

MARCUS AURELIUS

"The world turns aside to let any man pass who knows where he is going."

EPICTETUS

"You act like mortals in all that you fear and like immortals in all that you desire."

SENECA

"The obstacle on the path becomes the path. Never forget, within every obstacle is an opportunity to improve our condition."

MARCUS AURELIUS

"Your own will is all that you truly have."

EPICTETUS

"A man must stand erect, not be kept erect by others."

MARCUS AURELIUS

"Most powerful is he who has himself
in his own power."

"Difficulties are things that show a person
what they are."

"It is a rough road that leads to the heights of
greatness."

"Character is the only secure foundation
of the state."

"Your days are numbered. Use them to throw
open the windows of your soul to the sun. If you
do not, the sun will soon set, and you with it."

"All cruelty springs from weakness."

SENECA

"If a man could banish all fear of the gods and death and the fear of pain if he could realize that fate is a word without meaning, that nothing is ever created by divine will, that everything happens by chance... he would be marching on the road to true freedom."

SENECA

"Who then is invincible? The one who cannot be upset by anything outside their reasoned choice."

EPICTETUS

"There is no easy way from the earth to the stars, but we must not let the difficulty of the journey deter us. We must find solace in the climb itself and in the view that it affords."

SENECA

"Nothing will stand in the way of thy acting justly and soberly and considerately."

MARCUS AURELIUS

"It is the power of the mind to be unconquerable."

SENECA

"True peace is characterized by nothing so much as steadiness and imperturbability."

EPICTETUS

"All the terms of our human condition should be before our eyes."

SENECA

"On the occasion of every accident that befalls you, remember to turn to yourself and inquire what power you have for turning it to use."

EPICTETUS

"It is a rough road that leads to the heights of greatness."

SENECA

"You have to assemble your life yourself – action by action."

MARCUS AURELIUS

"The one who knows no hope knows no despair."

SENECA

"Begin each day by telling yourself: Today, I shall be meeting with interference, ingratitude, insolence, disloyalty, ill-will, and selfishness."

MARCUS AURELIUS

"Nothing is more honorable than a grateful heart."

SENECA

"Ignorance is the cause of fear."

SENECA

"Do every act of your life as if it
were your last."

MARCUS AURELIUS

"It is more necessary for the soul to be cured
than the body, for it is better to die
than to live badly."

MUSONIUS RUFUS

"No untroubled day has ever dawned
for the human race."

SENECA

"Man conquers the world by
conquering himself."

ZENO OF CITIUM

"For the only safe harbor in this life's tossing, the troubled sea is to refuse to be bothered about what the future will bring and to stand ready and confident, squaring the breast to take without skulking or flinching whatever fortune hurls at us."

SENECA

"If you seek truth, you will not seek victory by dishonorable means, and if you find truth, you will become invincible."

EPICTETUS

"We should always be prepared so that we never have to be prepared."

MUSONIUS RUFUS

"We should every night call ourselves to an account: What infirmity have I mastered today? What passions are opposed? What temptation resisted? What virtue acquired?"

SENECA

"You could leave life right now. Let that determine what you do and say and think."

MARCUS AURELIUS

"He who is brave is free."

SENECA

"Death smiles at us all, but all a man can do is smile back."

MARCUS AURELIUS

"You are invincible if nothing outside the will can disconcert you."

EPICTETUS

"Ask yourself at every moment, "Is this necessary?" But do not ask, "Is it possible to avoid this or that?" If you encounter difficulty, you will not be able to avoid it, but you will be able to endure it."

MARCUS AURELIUS

"The greatest of empires is the empire over one's self."

PUBLILIUS SYRUS (INFLUENCED BY STOICISM)

"He who fears death will always be a slave to anything that can save him from it. True freedom comes from accepting the inevitable and finding peace within it."

SENECA

"The greatest task of a person is to find meaning in pain and suffering. Our greatest test is not how we endure hardship, but how we make use of it."

SENECA

"Never esteem anything as of advantage to you that will make you break your word or lose your self-respect."

MARCUS AURELIUS

"It is not what we bear, but how we bear it, that matters."

SENECA

"The difficulty comes from our lack of confidence."

SENECA

"To be calm is the highest achievement of the self."

ZENO OF CITIUM

"No man is more unhappy than he who never faces adversity. For he is not permitted to prove himself."

SENECA

"Look well into thyself; there is a source of strength which will always spring up if thou wilt always look."

MARCUS AURELIUS

"Sometimes even to live is an act of courage."

SENECA

"The impediment to action advances action. What stands in the way becomes the way."

MARCUS AURELIUS

"For manliness gains much strength by being challenged."

SENECA

"Remember, it is not enough to be hit or insulted to be harmed; you must believe that you are being harmed. If someone succeeds in provoking you, realize that your mind is complicit in the provocation. This is why it is essential that we not respond impulsively to impressions; take a moment before reacting, and you will find it easier to maintain control."

EPICTETUS

"Fire tests gold, suffering tests brave men."

SENECA

"Why all this guesswork? You can see what needs to be done. If you can see the road, follow it."

MARCUS AURELIUS

"A man is as unhappy as he has convinced himself he is."

SENECA

"The greater the difficulty, the more glory in surmounting it. Skillful pilots gain their reputation from storms and tempests. "

EPICTETUS

"What we cannot bear removes us from life; what remains can be borne."

MARCUS AURELIUS

"Bravery is a scorner of things which inspire fear; it looks down upon, challenges, and crushes the powers of terror and all that would drive our freedom under the yoke."

EPICTETUS

"Brave men rejoice in adversity, just as brave soldiers triumph in war."

SENECA

"Let no act be done without a purpose."

MARCUS AURELIUS

"Excellence withers without an adversary."

SENECA

"You have the power of patience to deal with your difficulties."

EPICTETUS

JUSTICE

THE VIRTUE OF JUSTICE

Let's turn our attention to Justice, a cornerstone of Stoic philosophy that guides us in our interactions with others and the world. Justice, from a Stoic perspective, is not just about legal or societal norms; it's about our personal commitment to fairness, integrity, and the welfare of our community.

Justice in Stoicism is about doing the right thing, not just for ourselves, but for the greater good. It's about treating others with respect and fairness, regardless of their status or relationship to us. This virtue calls us to look beyond our personal desires and consider the impact of our actions on others and the world.

CULTIVATING JUSTICE IN EVERYDAY LIFE

How do we cultivate Justice in our daily lives? It begins with self-reflection and honesty. We must constantly evaluate our actions and intentions, asking ourselves if we are being fair and equitable. It's about listening to others, understanding their perspectives, and acting in a way that promotes harmony and understanding.

Stoicism teaches us rational Justice. This means making decisions based on reason and wisdom rather than emotion or personal gain. It involves considering the consequences of our actions and choosing the path that brings the most good to the most people.

At the heart of Justice is empathy. Understanding the experiences and feelings of others is crucial in making just decisions. It's about putting ourselves in others' shoes and acting with compassion and kindness.

Every day, we face choices that test our sense of Justice. Whether it's in our personal relationships, our work, or our role in society, we are constantly called to act justly. This might mean standing up for someone who is being treated unfairly, making ethical choices in our professional lives, or simply being honest and transparent in our dealings with others.

YOUR PERSONAL JOURNEY WITH JUSTICE

As you read through the quotes in this section, reflect on how they resonate with your understanding of Justice. Consider the areas in your life where you can practice more fairness and integrity. Remember, Justice is not about grandiose acts; it's about the everyday choices we make that collectively shape a just and equitable world.

Justice is about living with a sense of responsibility towards others and the world. It's a journey of constant learning, empathy, and the pursuit of fairness. Embrace this path of Justice, and let it guide you to a life of integrity, harmony, and a deep sense of fulfillment in contributing to the greater good.

"Nature has given man one tongue but two ears, that we may hear from others twice as much as we speak."

EPICTETUS

"Choose not to be harmed – and you won't feel harmed. Don't feel harmed – and you haven't been."

MARCUS AURELIUS

"If you wish to be loved, love."

SENECA

"There is nothing more inspiring than a speaker who makes clear to his audience that he has need of them."

EPICTETUS

"The best indication of a man's character is how he treats people who can't do him any good."

SENECA

"To do harm is to do yourself harm. To do an injustice is to do yourself an injustice – it degrades you."

MARCUS AURELIUS

"Happy is the man who can make others better, not merely when he is in their company, but even when he is in their thoughts!"

SENECA

"I have often wondered how it is that every man loves himself more than all the rest of men but yet sets less value on his own opinion of himself than on the opinion of others."

MARCUS AURELIUS

"Who are these people whose admiration you seek? Aren't they the ones you are used to describing as mad? Well, then, is that what you want – to be admired by the mad?"

EPICTETUS

"Wherever there is a human being, there is an opportunity for kindness."

SENECA

"Kindness is invincible, but only when it's sincere, not faking anything or putting on a show."

MARCUS AURELIUS

"A guide, on finding a man who has lost his way, brings him back to the right path – he does not mock and jeer at him and then take himself off. You also must show the unlearned man the truth, and you will see that he will follow. But so long as you do not show it to him, you should not mock but rather feel your own incapacity."

EPICTETUS

"He who laughs at the human race deserves better of it than he who mourns for it, for the former leaves it better hope of improvement."

SENECA

"Every pleasure is most valued when it is coming to an end?"

SENECA

"Whenever you are about to find fault with someone, ask yourself the following question: What fault of mine most nearly resembles the one I am about to criticize?"

MARCUS AURELIUS

"We live among wicked man through our own wickedness. One thing alone can bring us peace, an agreement to treat one another with kindness."

SENECA

"But when you are looking on anyone as a friend when you do not trust him as you trust yourself, you are making a grave mistake and have failed to grasp sufficiently the full force of true friendship."

SENECA

"If you wish to be good, first believe that you are bad."

EPICTETUS

"Be tolerant with others and strict with yourself."

MARCUS AURELIUS

"Natural ability without education has more often raised a man to glory and virtue than education without natural ability."

MARCUS AURELIUS

"If they are wise, do not quarrel with them; if they are fools, ignore them."

EPICTETUS

"All the good are friends of one another."

ZENO OF CITIUM

"The greatest remedy for anger is delay."

SENECA

"Live out your life in truth and justice, tolerant of those who are neither true nor just."

MARCUS AURELIUS

"It is not the actions of others which trouble us (for those actions are controlled by their governing part), but rather it is our own judgments. Therefore, remove those judgments and resolve to let go of your anger, and it will already be gone. How do you let go? By realizing that such actions are not shameful to you."

MARCUS AURELIUS

"For then thou wilt neither blame those who offend involuntarily nor wilt thou want their approbation if thou lookest to the sources of their opinions and appetites."

MARCUS AURELIUS

"It is difficult to bring people to goodness with lessons, but it is easy to do so by example."

SENECA

"When another blames you or hates you, or people voice similar criticisms, go to their souls, penetrate inside, and see what sort of people they are. You will realize that there is no need to be racked with anxiety that they should hold any particular opinion about you."

MARCUS AURELIUS

"It is unrealistic to expect people to see you as you see yourself."

EPICTETUS

"Never esteem of anything as profitable, which shall ever constrain thee either to break thy faith or to lose thy modesty; to hate any man, to suspect, to curse, to dissemble, to lust after anything, that requireth the secret of walls or veils."

MARCUS AURELIUS

"One of the most beautiful qualities of true friendship is to understand and to be understood."

SENECA

"A noble man compares and estimates himself by an idea which is higher than himself; and a mean man, by one lower than himself. The one produces aspiration; the other ambition, which is the way in which a vulgar man aspires."

MARCUS AURELIUS

"All those who engage you in their business disengage you from yourself."

SENECA

"Even as the Sun doth not wait for prayers and incantations to rise, but shines forth and is welcomed by all: so thou also wait not for clapping of hands and shouts and praise to do thy duty; nay, do good of thine own accord, and thou wilt be loved like the Sun."

EPICTETUS

"Whoever does wrong, wrongs himself; whoever does injustice, does it to himself, making himself evil."

MARCUS AURELIUS

"Small-minded people blame others. Ordinary people blame themselves. The wise see all blame as foolishness."

EPICTETUS

"Dig within. Within is the wellspring of Good, and it is always ready to bubble up, if you just dig."

MARCUS AURELIUS

"To accuse others for one's own misfortune is a sign of want of education. To accuse oneself shows that one's education has begun. To accuse neither oneself nor others shows that one's education is complete."

EPICTETUS

"A person teaching and a person learning," he said, "Should have the same end in view: the improvement of the latter."

SENECA

"If you desire to be good, begin by believing that you are wicked."

EPICTETUS

"To understand the true quality of people, you must look into their minds and examine their pursuits and aversions."

MARCUS AURELIUS

"I have never wished to cater to the crowd, for what I know, they do not approve, and what they approve, I do not know."

SENECA

"How rotten and spurious is the man who says: "I have decided to be straightforward with you."

MARCUS AURELIUS

"For mankind, evil is injustice and cruelty and indifference to a neighbor's trouble, while virtue is brotherly love and goodness and justice and beneficence and concern for the welfare of your neighbor."

MUSONIUS RUFUS

"Don't imagine that something is good for you if, in pursuing it, you must break a promise, harm anyone else, lose self-respect, act hypocritically, or hide in shame."

MARCUS AURELIUS

"Everything has two handles, the one by which it may be carried, the other by which it cannot. If your brother acts unjustly, don't lay hold of the action by the handle of his injustice, for by that it cannot be carried; but by the opposite, that he is your brother, that you were brought up together, and then you will be carrying it by the handle that it can be carried."

EPICTETUS

"Humans have come into being for the sake of each other, so either teach them or learn to bear them."

MARCUS AURELIUS

"Never depend on the admiration of others. There is no strength in it. Personal merit cannot be derived from an external source. It is not to be found in your personal associations, nor can it be found in the regard of other people. It is a fact of life that other people, even people who love you, will not necessarily agree with your ideas, understand you, or share your enthusiasm. Grow up! Who cares what other people think about you!"

EPICTETUS

"No school has more goodness and gentleness; none has more love for human beings, nor more attention to the common good."

MUSONIUS RUFUS

"Life is neither good nor evil, but only
a place for good and evil."

MARCUS AURELIUS

"You can tell the character of every man when
you see how he receives praise."

SENECA

"Preach not to others what they should eat, but
eat as becomes you and be silent."

EPICTETUS

"Though you break your heart, men will go on
as before."

MARCUS AURELIUS

"It is shameful to hate a person who deserves
your praises, but how much more shameful it is
to hate someone for the very cause that makes
him deserve your pity."

SENECA

"If they've made a mistake, correct them gently and show them where they went wrong. If you can't do that, then the blame lies with you. Or no one."

MARCUS AURELIUS

"We should not blame the gods for the misfortunes of the wicked, for they bring them upon themselves by their own actions."

CHRYSIPPUS

"With each person you meet, remind yourself that you share a common humanity. You are members of the same family. They may not know this, but you do – so show them by the way you treat them."

MARCUS AURELIUS

"Epictetus, being asked how a man should give pain to his enemy answered by preparing himself to live the best life that he could."

EPICTETUS

"They contemn one another, and yet they seek to please one another: and whilst they seek to surpass one another in worldly pomp and greatness, they most debase and prostitute themselves in their better part one to another."

MARCUS AURELIUS

"Only an absolute fool values a man according to his clothes, or accord-ing to his social position, which after all is only something that we wear like clothing."

SENECA

"Adapt yourself to the life you have been given, and truly love the people with whom destiny has surrounded you."

MARCUS AURELIUS

"Don't expect to tell others what they should do when they know that you do what you shouldn't."

MUSONIUS RUFUS

"If someone tried to take control of your body and make you a slave, you would fight for freedom. Yet, how easily you hand over your mind to anyone who insults you. When you dwell on their words and let them dominate your thoughts, you make them your master."

EPICTETUS

"A man who makes a decision without listening to both sides is unjust, even if his ruling is a fair one."

SENECA

"If evil be said of thee, and if it be true, correct thyself; if it be a lie, laugh at it."

EPICTETUS

"If any man despises me, that is his problem. My only concern is not doing or saying anything deserving of contempt."

MARCUS AURELIUS

"If anyone tells you that a certain person speaks ill of you, do not make excuses about what is said of you but answer, "He was ignorant of my other faults; otherwise, he would not have mentioned these alone."

EPICTETUS

"Accept the things to which fate binds you, and love the people with whom fate brings you together, but do so with all your heart."

MARCUS AURELIUS

"The duty of a man is to be useful to his fellow men; if possible, to be useful to many of them; failing this, to be useful to a few; failing this, to be useful to his neighbors, and, failing them, to himself: for when he helps others, he advances the general interests of mankind.

SENECA

"He who laughs at himself never runs out of things to laugh at."

EPICTETUS

"The ambitious supposeth another man's act, praise and applause, to be his own happiness; the voluptuous his own sense and feeling; but he that is wise, his own action."

MARCUS AURELIUS

"I myself think that the wise man meddles little or not at all in affairs and does his own things."

CHRYSIPPUS

"The only thing that isn't worthless is to live this life out truthfully and rightly. And be patient with those who don't."

MARCUS AURELIUS

"Other people's views and troubles can be contagious. Don't sabotage yourself by unwittingly adopting negative, unproductive attitudes through your associations with others."

EPICTETUS

"It is ridiculous not to escape from one's own vices, which is possible while trying to escape the vices of others, which is impossible."

MARCUS AURELIUS

"Associate with those who will make a better man of you. Welcome those whom you yourself can improve. The process is mutual, for men learn while they teach."

SENECA

"I laugh at those who think they can damage me. They do not know who I am; they do not know what I think; they cannot even touch the things which are really mine and with which I live."

EPICTETUS

"There is no enjoying the possession of anything valuable unless one has someone to share it with."

SENECA

"You have no assurance that they are doing wrong at all, for the motives of man's actions are not always what they seem. There is generally much to learn before any judgment can be pronounced with certainty on another's doings."

MARCUS AURELIUS

"To accept injury without a spirit of savage resentment to show ourselves merciful toward those who wrong us being a source of good hope to them is characteristic of a benevolent and civilized way of life."

MUSONIUS RUFUS

"To feel affection for people even when they make mistakes is uniquely human."

MARCUS AURELIUS

"Do not try to seem wise to others. If you want to live a wise life, live it on your own terms and in your own eyes."

EPICTETUS

"People find pleasure in different ways. I find it in keeping my mind clear. In not turning away from people or the things that happen to them. In accepting and welcoming everything I see."

MARCUS AURELIUS

"Never wilt your soul; never be just good, simple, or unpolished. Manifest more than the body that surrounds yourself."

MARCUS AURELIUS

"He who is running a race ought to endeavor and strive to the utmost of his ability to come off victor, but it is utterly wrong for him to trip up his competitor or to push him aside. So, in life, it is not unfair for one to seek for himself what may accrue to his benefit, but it is not right to take it from another."

CHRYSIPPUS

"When men are inhuman, take care not to feel towards them as they do towards other humans."

MARCUS AURELIUS

"Whenever anyone criticizes or wrongs you, remember that they are only doing or saying what they think is right. They cannot be guided by your views, only their own, so if their views are wrong, they are the ones who suffer insofar as they are misguided."

EPICTETUS

"Humanity is the quality which stops one being arrogant towards one's fellows or being acrimonious."

SENECA

"It is in our power to have no opinion about a thing and not to be disturbed in our soul, for things themselves have no natural power to form our judgments."

MARCUS AURELIUS

"A wise man never asks what another man serves, for only his actions will speak the truth."

SENECA

"Other people's mistakes? Leave them
to their makers."

MARCUS AURELIUS

"To admonish is better than to reproach, for
admonition is mild and friendly, but reproach is
harsh and insulting, and admonition corrects
those who are doing wrong, but reproach only
convicts them."

EPICTETUS

"The man who tries to find out what has been
said against him, who seeks to unearth spiteful
gossip, even when engaged in privately, is
destroying his own peace of mind."

SENECA

"A good man does not spy around for the black
spots in others but presses unswervingly on
towards his mark."

MARCUS AURELIUS

"No matter how good a life you lead, you won't please everyone."

MARCUS AURELIUS

"Try to enjoy the great festival of life with other men."

EPICTETUS

"I imagine many people could have achieved wisdom if they had not imagined they had already achieved it if they had not dissembled about some of their own characteristics and turned a blind eye to others."

SENECA

"And you can also commit injustice by doing nothing."

MARCUS AURELIUS

"Blame and praise have no true effects."

MARCUS AURELIUS

"If you must be affected by other people's misfortunes, show them pity instead of contempt. Drop this readiness to hate and take offense."

EPICTETUS

"But nothing delights the mind so much as fond and loyal friendship. What a blessing it is to have hearts that are ready and willing to receive all your secretes in safety, with whom you are less afraid to share knowledge of something than keep it to yourself, whose conversation soothes your distress, whose advice helps you make up your mind, whose cheerfulness dissolves your sorrow, whose very appearance
cheers you up!"

SENECA

"The things ordained for you – teach yourself to be at one with those. And the people who share them with you – treat them with love.
With real love."

MARCUS AURELIUS

"When you are offended at any man's fault, turn to yourself and study your own failings. Then you will forget your anger."

EPICTETUS

"Not to be offended with other men's liberty of speech."

MARCUS AURELIUS

"For we are made for co-operation, like feet, hands, eyelids, like the rows of the upper and lower teeth. To act against one another then is contrary to nature, and it is acting against one another to be vexed and to turn away."

MARCUS AURELIUS

"No one can live happily who has regard for himself alone and transforms everything into a question of his own utility."

SENECA

"It is not fit that I should give myself pain, for I have never intentionally given pain
even to another."

MARCUS AURELIUS

"Whenever you act from clear judgment, doing what needs to be done, do not worry about what others will think – even if the whole world might misunderstand you."

EPICTETUS

"In a sense, people are our proper occupation. Our job is to do them good and
put up with them."

MARCUS AURELIUS

"When you are offended at any man's fault, immediately turn to yourself and reflect in what manner you yourself have erred."

MARCUS AURELIUS

"When you are feeling upset, angry, or sad, don't blame another for your state of mind."

"Goodness exists independently of our conception of it. The good is out there, and it always has been out there, even before we began to exist."

"Justice: so that you'll speak the truth, frankly and without evasions, and act as you should – and as other people deserve."

MARCUS AURELIUS

"A boxer derives the greatest advantage from his sparring partner – and my accuser is my sparring partner. He trains me in patience, civility, and even temper."

EPICTETUS

TEMPERANCE

THE VIRTUE OF TEMPERANCE

We arrive at Temperance, a virtue that speaks to the heart of self-mastery and balance. Temperance, in the Stoic sense, is about moderation, self-control, and the disciplined use of our resources, be it time, energy, or even emotions.

Temperance is often misunderstood as mere abstinence or denial, but it's much more in Stoicism. It's about finding the right measure in all aspects of life. It's not just about restraining ourselves from overindulgence in pleasures but also about managing our desires, emotions, and actions in a balanced, rational manner.

THE ROLE OF TEMPERANCE IN DAILY LIFE

Every day, we are bombarded with choices and temptations that test our self-control. In a world of excess, practicing Temperance means making conscious decisions that align with our values and long-term goals rather than succumbing to fleeting desires or impulses.

Temperance is the balancing act between our desires and our duties. It's about prioritizing what truly matters and making choices that reflect our deepest values. This virtue teaches us to enjoy life's pleasures, but not at the cost of our responsibilities or our moral and ethical standards.

One of the great paradoxes of Temperance is that in exercising self-control, we actually gain more freedom. By not being slaves to our impulses or desires, we gain the freedom to choose our path, to live in alignment with our principles, and to pursue a life of meaning and purpose.

How do we cultivate this virtue in our daily lives? It starts with mindfulness – being aware of our impulses and desires and questioning whether they serve our higher goals. It involves setting boundaries for ourselves and sticking to them, even when it's challenging. It's about finding joy in simplicity and learning to be content with what we have.

YOUR PERSONAL JOURNEY WITH TEMPERANCE

As you delve into the quotes in this section, reflect on how Temperance plays a role in your life. Are there areas where you could practice more self-control? How can you find a healthier balance in your daily routines, relationships, and personal goals?

Remember, Temperance is not about denying yourself the joys of life; it's about enjoying them in a way that is sustainable, responsible, and in harmony with your true self. It's a journey of constant learning and growth, where each step towards self-control is a step towards a more fulfilled and balanced life.

In embracing Temperance, you embrace a life of balance, wisdom, and inner peace. It's a path that leads not just to self-improvement but to a deeper understanding and appreciation of the world around you. Let this virtue guide you in your choices and actions, and watch as it transforms your life into one of harmony and profound satisfaction.

"True happiness is to enjoy the present, without anxious dependence upon the future, not to amuse ourselves with either hopes or fears but to rest satisfied with what we have, which is sufficient."

SENECA

"Wealth consists not in having great possessions, but in having few wants."

EPICTETUS

"The contented man is never poor, the discontented never rich."

EPICTETUS

"No person has the power to have everything they want, but it is in their power not to want what they don't have and to cheerfully put to good use what they do have."

SENECA

"Make the best use of what is in your power, and take the rest as it happens."

EPICTETUS

"Receive without conceit, release without struggle."

MARCUS AURELIUS

"Remember that you must behave in life as at a dinner party. Is anything brought around to you? Put out your hand and take your share with moderation. Does it pass by you? Don't stop it. Has it not yet come? Don't stretch your desire towards it, but wait till it reaches you."

EPICTETUS

"He is a wise man who does not grieve for the things which he has not but rejoices for those which he has."

EPICTETUS

"It is not the man who has too little, but the man who craves more that is poor."

"Very little is needed to make a happy life; it is all within yourself, in your way of thinking."

"He suffers more than necessary, who suffers before it is necessary."

"He has the most who is content with the least."

"If you live in harmony with nature, you will never be poor; if you live according to what others think, you will never be rich."

"We ought always to deal justly, not only with those who are just to us but likewise to those who endeavor to injure us; and this, for fear lest by rendering them evil for evil, we should fall into the same vice."

HIEROCLES

"If you want to improve, be content to be thought foolish and stupid. Embrace the simplicity of life, and do not be swayed by the opinions and criticisms of others."

EPICTETUS

"The only wealth which you will keep forever is the wealth you have given away."

MARCUS AURELIUS

"Freedom is secured not by the fulfilling of one's desires, but by the removal of desire."

EPICTETUS

"No one can lose either the past or the future –
how could anyone be deprived of what he does
not possess? ... It is only the present moment of
which either stands to be deprived, and if this is
all he has, he cannot lose what he does not have."

MARCUS AURELIUS

"The greatest blessings of mankind are within
us and within our reach."

SENECA

"All things fade and quickly turn to myth."

MARCUS AURELIUS

"A person's worth is measured by the worth
of what he values."

MARCUS AURELIUS

"Wealth is the slave of a wise man.
The master of a fool."

SENECA

"If reason tells you pleasure is wholesome and harmless, you may enjoy it in moderation. But take care not to let your happiness gradually become dependent on it."

EPICTETUS

"Do not be ashamed of help."

MARCUS AURELIUS

"A companion's crudeness is bound to rub off on the one he is with, no matter how refined that person may be."

EPICTETUS

"Well-being is attained by little and little, and nevertheless is no little thing itself."

ZENO OF CITIUM

"The sun also shines on the wicked."

SENECA

"Do not seek to have everything that happens happen as you wish, but wish for everything to happen as it actually does happen, and your life will be serene."

EPICTETUS

"And he who pursues pleasure will not abstain from injustice, and this is plainly impiety."

MARCUS AURELIUS

"I am content with few, content with one, content with none at all."

SENECA

"A man should so live that his happiness shall depend as little as possible on external things."

EPICTETUS

"Don't cling to possessions and other external things; cling only to the divine spark within you."

MARCUS AURELIUS

"No one can have a peaceful life who thinks too much about lengthening it."

SENECA

"Those who are able to control their passions instead of letting their passions control them are free."

EPICTETUS

"For many men, the acquisition of wealth does not end their troubles; it only changes them."

SENECA

"Do not seek the things that are too high for you. The best indication of wisdom is to see what is right in front of you."

MUSONIUS RUFUS

"Everything which went beyond our actual needs was just so much unnecessary weight, a burden to the man who had to carry it."

SENECA

"The foundation of happiness is to understand that desire and aversion are within our power. Desire what you can control and avert what you cannot control."

EPICTETUS

"Kindness is unconquerable, so long as it is without flattery or hypocrisy. For what can the most insolent man do to you if you contrive to be kind to him, and if you have the chance, gently advise and calmly show him what is right...and point this out tactfully and from a universal perspective. But you must not do this with sarcasm or reproach, but lovingly and without anger in your soul."

MARCUS AURELIUS

"Only the wise man is content with what is his. All foolishness suffers the burden of dissatisfaction with itself."

SENECA

"So, if you have not been invited to a party, it is because you haven't paid the price of the invitation. It costs social engagement, conversation, encouragement, and praise. If you are not willing to pay this price, do not be upset when you don't receive an invitation."

EPICTETUS

"Wise people want nothing yet need many things. On the other hand, nothing is needed by fools, for they do not understand how to use anything but are in want of everything."

CHRYSIPPUS

"Enjoy present pleasures in such a way as not to injure future ones."

SENECA

"Circumstances do not rise to meet our expectations. Events happen as they do. People behave as they are. Embrace what you actually get."

EPICTETUS

"Let us train our minds to desire what the situation demands. Instead of wishing for what we do not have, let us cherish and make the best use of the things we do have."

SENECA

"People are frugal in guarding their personal property, but as soon as it comes to squandering time, they are most wasteful of the one thing in which it is right to be stingy."

SENECA

"Accept whatever comes to you woven in the pattern of your destiny, for what could more aptly fit your needs?"

MARCUS AURELIUS

"We are at the mercy of whoever wields authority over the things we either desire or detest. If you would be free, then do not wish to have, or avoid, things that other people control because then you must serve as their slave."

EPICTETUS

"A gift consists not in what is done or given,
but in the intention of the giver or doer."

SENECA

"Do not indulge in dreams of having what you
have not, but reckon up the chief of the blessings
you do possess, and then thankfully remember
how you would crave for them if
they were not yours."

MARCUS AURELIUS

"You ask what is the proper limit to a person's
wealth? First, having what is essential, and
second, having what is enough."

SENECA

"Until we have begun to go without them, we
fail to realize how unnecessary many things are.
We've been using them not because we needed
them but because we had them."

SENECA

"We will train both soul and body when we accustom ourselves to cold, heat, thirst, hunger, scarcity of food, hardness of bed, abstaining from pleasures, and enduring pains."

MUSONIUS RUFUS

"However much you possess, there's someone else who has more, and you'll be fancying yourself to be short of things you need to the exact extent to which you lag behind him."

SENECA

"Neither worse than or better is a thing made by being praised."

MARCUS AURELIUS

"When Zeno received news of a shipwreck and heard that all his luggage had been sunk, he said, "Fortune bids me to be a less encumbered philosopher."

SENECA

"Be the same person in public as in private."

"I do not regard a man as poor if the little which remains is enough for him."

MARCUS AURELIUS

"The boon that could be given can be withdrawn."

SENECA

"Almost nothing material is needed for a happy life, for he who has understood existence."

MARCUS AURELIUS

"Be silent as to services you have rendered, but speak of favors you have received."

SENECA

"But I'll get money and then share it." If you can acquire riches without losing your honor and self-respect, then do it. But if you lose what is dearest to you, no amount of money can make up for it."

EPICTETUS

"Let us take pleasure in what we have received and make no comparison; no man will ever be happy if tortured by the greater happiness of another."

SENECA

"What, then, is your own? The way you live your life."

EPICTETUS

"None of those who have been raised to a loftier height by riches and honors is really great."

EPICTETUS

"Asked, "Who is the rich man?" Epictetus replied, "He who is content.""

EPICTETUS

"Think for a long time whether or not you should admit a given person to your friendship. But when you have decided to do so, welcome his heart and soul and speak as unreservedly with him as you would with yourself."

SENECA

"Try how the good man's life suits thee, the life of him who is satisfied with his portion out of the whole and satisfied with his own just acts and benevolent disposition."

MARCUS AURELIUS

"You've given aid, and they've received it. And yet, like an idiot, you keep holding out for more: to be credited with a Good Deed, to be repaid in kind. Why?"

MARCUS AURELIUS

"If you gape after externals, you must, of necessity, ramble up and down in obedience to the will of your master. And who is the master? He who has the power over the things which you seek to gain or try to avoid."

EPICTETUS

ACKNOWLEDGEMENTS

Dear Reader,

As we conclude this journey through the pages of this book, I find myself filled with a deep sense of gratitude. Your time and encouragement in reading these words have been a source of immense support and inspiration for me. This connection, this shared exploration of life's wisdom, propels me forward to continue sharing my experiences in future writings.

I am profoundly thankful to my wife and children, whose unwavering support has been a cornerstone of my strength and perseverance. Their belief in my vision has been a guiding light, illuminating the path through challenges and triumphs. Equally, my heartfelt gratitude extends to my friends, whose support and wise counsel have been invaluable.

My sincerest hope is that you, dear Reader, have found valuable insights within these pages. May the Stoic quotes and philosophies serve as tools for you to craft a world that resonates with your deepest values and aspirations. Remember, It is in your power to create and transform your life that lies within your hands.

I wholeheartedly recommend my book *Stoicism for New Life* for you to embrace the teachings of Stoicism not just as a concept but as a life practice. Small habits and consistent actions lead to profound changes. Integrate them into the fabric of your daily life, and watch as they bring about a transformation in your world.

Create your life with intention, courage, and resilience. And most importantly, always move forward on this path of growth and self-discovery.

With heartfelt thanks and best wishes for your journey,
Michael Whiteclear

Printed in Great Britain
by Amazon